CHOPIN IN MANCHESTER

[Plate 1] Frederick Chopin (1810–49)
Stanisław Stattler (1858), based on portrait by Ary Scheffer, *c.*1847 (destroyed)
Print from the 'Corpus Imaginum' of the Photographic Society

PETER WILLIS

CHOPIN
in Manchester

Elysium Press Publishers

Newcastle upon Tyne 2011

For Jenny, Magnus, Gemma, Imogen and Erin

Published by Elysium Press Publishers
5 Fenwick Close · Jesmond · Newcastle upon Tyne NE2 2LE · UK
First printing 2011 in an edition of 1,000 copies

ISBN 978 0 904712 05 6

This publication is a revised version of the article
'Chopin's Recital in the Gentlemen's Concert Hall,
Monday 28 August 1848', published in *Manchester Sounds,*
volume 8 (2009–10), pp.84–119,
the journal of the Manchester Musical Heritage Trust,
generously supported by the Ida Carroll Trust

Typeset by Martin Thacker
Designed by Dalrymple
Printed in Poland by OZGraf SA

Front cover: Detail of bronze statue of Chopin by Ludwika Nitschowa
(1889–1989). Gift of Frederick Chopin Society of Poland to the
Royal Northern College of Music, Manchester, 1973, to mark the
125th anniversary of Chopin's concert in the city in 1848
Courtesy Royal Northern College of Music, Manchester
Photograph: Michael Pollard, 2010

CONTENTS

PREFACE

CHOPIN IN MANCHESTER was first published as 'Chopin's Recital in the Gentlemen's Concert Hall, Monday 28 August 1848', in volume 8 of *Manchester Sounds* (2009–10), the journal of the Manchester Musical Heritage Trust. I am grateful to David Fallows, Editor of *Manchester Sounds*, and John Turner, Chairman of the Manchester Musical Heritage Trust, for consenting to the appearance of the article as a separate publication.

The text was typeset by Martin Thacker, and the book designed by Robert Dalrymple, of the Edinburgh firm Dalrymple. I am greatly indebted to them both. Ian Chilvers gave invaluable help with the proofs and, as always, the contribution of the editorial and production staff of Elysium Press has been indispensable.

On 16 September 2011, after *Chopin in Manchester* went to press, a bronze statue of Chopin seated at a piano, by the Polish sculptor Robert Sobociński, was unveiled outside Centurion House, Deansgate, in central Manchester.

Jeremy Dibble provided support and encouragement in my research on Chopin over many years.

My greatest debt is to my wife Jenny, and our family, to whom the following pages are affectionately dedicated.

PETER WILLIS

family firm of *Pleyel et Cie* manufactured Chopin's favourite pianos. Chopin visited the piano manufacturer James Shudi Broadwood and his family at 46 Bryanston Square, using the pseudonym 'M. Fritz', went to the opera, saw the sights, and signed contracts with his publisher, Wessel. Chopin kept his presence low-key. On 1 September 1837, Mendelssohn remarked to Ferdinand Hiller that 'Chopin came over quite suddenly a fortnight ago, paid no visits and saw nobody, played very beautifully at Broadwood's one evening, and then took himself off again. They say he is still very ill and miserable.'[3] In like vein, Moscheles refers in his diary to the composer's visit. 'Chopin', he wrote, 'who spent a few days in London, was the only one of the foreign artists who did not go out, and wished no one to visit him, for the effort of talking told on his consumptive frame. He heard a few concerts and disappeared.'[4]

In 1848 it was a different story, although Chopin continued to suffer from ill health. Once in London, he was caught up in a round of activity. He took rooms in 48 Dover Street, near Piccadilly, resumed his teaching, and gave recitals in elegant domestic settings such as Stafford House (now Lancaster House) for the Duke and Duchess of Sutherland on 15 May, when the guests included Queen Victoria and Prince Albert; he performed at Gore House in Kensington for Lady Blessington on 10 May, at 99 Eaton Place for Mrs Adelaide Sartoris on 23 June, and at 2 St James's Square for the Earl of Falmouth on 7 July. He was also entertained, among others, by the Broadwood family, by Thomas and Jane Welsh Carlyle at 5 (later renumbered 24) Cheyne Row, by H. F. Chorley at 15 Victoria Square, by Mrs George Grote (biographer of Scheffer) at 12 Savile Row, and by William Stirling at 39 Clarges Street.[5]

Although tickets were sold for the recitals at Mrs Sartoris' and the Earl of Falmouth's, their settings were domestic rather than public, and it was only when he reached Scotland that Chopin performed in concert halls. On 5 August, accompanied by the musician and photographer John Muir Wood, he took the train from Euston to Edinburgh, where he was met by the Stirlings' Polish physician Dr Adam Lyschiński, a homeopath, with whom he stayed at 10 Warriston Crescent. Subsequently, Chopin was a guest at Scottish country houses, seats of aristocratic families often related to Jane Stirling – notably Calder House (Lord Torphichen), Johnstone Castle (the Houstons), Strachur (the Murrays), Wishaw (the Belhavens), Keir (William Stirling), Milliken (the Napiers), and Hamilton Palace (the Hamiltons). Apart from playing privately for his Scottish hosts, Chopin gave three public concerts during this time: the first (which

[Plate 2] London Road, Manchester, showing London Road Station
in the centre at the top of the ramp
Painting by Arthur Fitzwilliam Tait, *c.*1844–50
Manchester City Galleries

took him briefly back to England) in Manchester, the second at the
Merchants' Hall in Glasgow, and the third at the Hopetoun Rooms
in Edinburgh.[6]

Chopin's most prominent host in Scotland was Lord Torphichen,
who entertained him at Calder House, near Edinburgh. On 19 August
1848, barely two weeks after his arrival in Scotland, Chopin was writing
from Calder and telling his family in Warsaw of his forthcoming concert in Manchester, 'at which Italians from London will sing' and for
which he was to be paid £60, 'which is not to be turned down'. He was
to travel the 200 miles from Edinburgh by train, which, he noted, was
a journey of eight hours.[7] In all likelihood this would have taken him
on the Caledonian Railway to Carlisle, where he would have changed
to the London & North Western Railway, arriving either at Salford
Station, New Bailey Street, or at London Road Station, now known
as Piccadilly [plate 2].[8]

It goes without saying that Manchester, bustling industrial city and centre of commerce [plate 3], had a lively musical life.[9] In Manchester, Chopin explains,

> *some kind friends are awaiting me, wealthy manufacturers who have Neukomm staying with them. (He was Haydn's best pupil and used to be court conductor to the Emperor of Brazil – you must have heard his name.) They have also Mrs Rich, daughter of Mr Mackintosh, a highly esteemed man who was a Member of Parliament – he is a speaker and writer. She is a great friend of both myself and the Stirlings and Erskines.*[10]

The 'kind friends' were Salis Schwabe and his wife Julie Schwabe, who had recently moved from Rusholme House, on the southern outskirts of Manchester, to Crumpsall House, to the north of the city [plates 4, 5].[11] Crumpsall was a classical mansion with outbuildings, set in open landscape with a prominent lake; it has since been demolished to make way for a housing estate.[12] Jenny Lind (1820–87), the soprano nicknamed 'the Swedish nightingale' [plate 16], was also a friend of the Schwabes, and the previous year had made her first appearances

[Plate 3] View of Manchester
Engraving by C. Reiss, Hildburghausen, *c.*1842

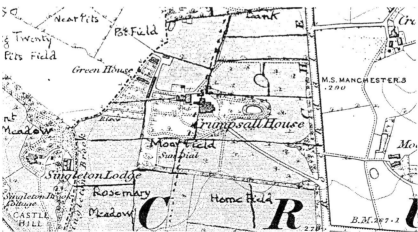

[Plate 4] Crumpsall House, Greater Manchester
Undated photograph from Susanna Brookshaw, *Concerning Chopin in Manchester* (Manchester, 1937; repr. 1951), frontispiece

[Plate 5] Crumpsall House, Greater Manchester
Detail from Ordnance Survey, 6 inches to 1 mile, *c.*1847–8 (sheet 96)

[Plate 6] Salis Schwabe (1800–53)
Bust by William Bally, *c.*1853
Old Grammar School, Middleton, Greater Manchester

in Manchester: on 28 August 1847 as Amina in *La sonnambula*, and on
2 September as Maria in Donizetti's *La figlia del reggimento*. Between
these performances, on 31 August, reports William Axon, 'she was
serenaded by the Liedertafel at Rusholme House, the residence of Mrs.
Salis Schwabe, whose guest she was'. Engagingly, during her stay Lind
'was often seen riding on horseback in the direction of Didsbury'.[13]
She visited Manchester once more in 1848, appearing as Lucia in *Lucia
di Lammermoor* on 9 September, and again as Amina two days later. In
this, and in her preceding visit in 1847, she was supported by the Italian
bass Luigi Lablache.[14]

Salis Schwabe's likeness, in a toga, can be seen in a bust by William Bally [plate 6],[15] and his wife's in a fine portrait by Ary Scheffer [plate 7].[16] Bally (*fl.* 1829–56) was a phrenologist and sculptor, born in Switzerland. In the 1830s and 1840s he ran the phrenological gallery in King Street, Manchester, and in 1838 served as curator of the Manchester Phrenological Society. Scheffer (1795–1858), the Dutch painter, engraver and book illustrator, spent most of his career in Paris, where he had many friends among musicians and Polish émigrés. Those entertained in his Parisian salon included Chopin, Delacroix, Franchomme, Liszt, George Sand and Pauline Viardot.[17]

Salis Schwabe and his brother Adolf ran a calico factory at Rhodes, Middleton, outside Manchester. Chopin knew the Schwabes from

[Plate 7] Julie Schwabe (1819–96)
Portrait by Ary Scheffer, 1850–1
Froebel Archive for Childhood Studies, Roehampton University

[Plate 8] Chopin. Autograph of song 'Wiosna', with Polish words by Stefan Witwicki, inscribed '*souvenir de Crumpsal House / à Mademoiselle Fanny Erskine / F Chopin*', and dated 1 September 1848 (MU.MS.679.f.13r)
Fitzwilliam Museum, Cambridge

cultural life in Paris, where they consorted with Auguste and Sophie Léo, Fanny Erskine, Hallé, Jane Stirling, Mrs Katherine Erskine, Mrs Mary Rich and musicians such as Thomas Tellefsen.[18] Chopin has given us a thumbnail sketch of the Schwabes. Writing to his close friend Wojciech Gryzmała, the Polish man of letters, he explained that when in Manchester he

> lived in the suburbs as there is too much smoke in the town: all the rich people have their houses outside the town. I was staying with my good friend Schwabe – you may have seen him at Léo's. He is a leading manufacturer and owns the tallest chimney in Manchester – it cost him £5,000. He is a friend of Cobden's and a great free-trader himself. He is a Jew – or rather a Protestant convert like Léo. His wife is particularly kind. They insisted on my staying longer, as Jenny Lind is arriving there this week and will also be staying with them.

Chopin added that the Schwabes and Jenny Lind 'are great friends'. 'While I was there', he continued, 'we also had that dear Mrs Rich whom you saw at my place with Miss Stirling'. He also saw Hermann Léo's brother, Auguste Léo, who was in Manchester 'on business'.[19]

Sigismund Neukomm, the Austrian composer, pianist and scholar, lived with the Schwabes for several months during the late summer and autumn of 1848, and he and Chopin seem to have been there together.[20] Among those whom Chopin encountered in Manchester, possibly at the Schwabes', was Fanny Erskine, to whom he gave a manuscript of the song 'Wiosna', inscribed *'souvenir de Crumpsal House / à Mademoiselle Fanny Erskine / F Chopin / 1, Sept. 1848'* [plate 8]. The date here indicates that Chopin did not leave Manchester until early September;[21] a day or two later, on 4 September, he was writing to Grzymała from Johnstone Castle, near Glasgow.[22]

The Schwabes entertained either at Crumpsall, or at Glyn Garth, Llandegfan, Isle of Anglesey, their house overlooking the Menai Strait [plate 9]; the prospect from Llandegfan has been called 'one of the grandest views in all Wales'.[23] This essay in a neo-Elizabethan style was built (at a cost of £40,000, it is said) by the Manchester architect John Edgar Gregan (1813–55).[24] Gregan specialised in ecclesiastical and commercial buildings, in a variety of styles including Puginian and Romanesque; in central Manchester, Renaissance palazzi provided inspiration for warehouses for Robert Barbour and Thomas Ashton, a bank for Sir Benjamin Heywood, in St Ann's Street (1848, now the Royal Bank of Scotland), and the Mechanics' Institute, in Princess Street (1854–5, now the National Museum of Labour History). At Glyn Garth, Gregan provided grandiose interiors which included a neo-medieval galleried hall and, it seems, work by the Crace firm of decorators. Between 1900 and 1925 the house was the official residence of the Bishop of Bangor and known as Glyn Garth Palace. Prior to its demolition in about 1964, to make way for a ten-storey block of flats named Glyn Garth Court, it was owned by the Friendship Holiday Association [plate 10].[25]

Chopin's description of the Schwabes does not do justice to the remarkable Julie Schwabe who, following her husband's death in 1853, carried on her cultural and philanthropic activities before moving to Naples, where she launched a one-woman campaign to raise funds to establish schools. Widowed at the age of thirty-four, Julie was left with seven children and a huge fortune. She was called 'a prophetess of liberal education', with a strong sense of social justice, and was involved in the Froebel movement of children's education. 'The Schwabe household was Unitarian', writes Peter Weston, 'and became a centre of enlightened Liberalism … They were advocates of democracy, or at least of encouraging working men, by hard work, thrift and education, to achieve the franchise.'[26] Friends and visitors, in Manchester and at Glyn Garth, included not only the radicals John Bright and

GLYN GARTH-MENAI STRAITS.

Published by T. Catherall, Chester & Bangor.

[Plate 9] Glyn Garth, Anglesey
John Edgar Gregan, architect, c.1850
View from the Menai Strait, published by Thomas Catherall, c.1860

[Plate 10] Glyn Garth, Anglesey, as Family Holiday Association guest house
View from the Menai Strait
Twentieth-century postcard (pre-c.1964)

Richard Cobden, but also Mrs Gaskell and the prison reformer Thomas Wright.[27] Malwida von Meysenbug, friend of Nietzsche and Wagner, and later author of *Memoiren einer Idealistin* (1876), among other works, made several visits to Glyn Garth and observed the Schwabe household's imitation of the manners and habits of the English aristocracy, noting that Salis Schwabe 'had the petty vanity of the parvenu and felt flattered in associating with the nobility'.[28] Geraldine Jewsbury visited the Schwabes frequently in 1848–9, writes Edward Morris, 'to hear her friend Sigismond Neukomm play the organ'. Additionally the 'Schwabes provided the link between the Manchester cotton manufacturers as patrons and collectors of Scheffer and Scheffer's English political and literary admirers'.[29] As such, they were part of a wide community of supporters of French art.[30]

THE GENTLEMEN'S CONCERT HALL

Chopin's Manchester recital took place in the Concert Hall, the venue used by the Gentlemen's Concert Society, which was founded in Manchester in 1777.[31] As Benjamin Love wrote, in *The Hand-Book of Manchester* (1842):

> *There are six hundred subscribers at five guineas, who have each two tickets, one for his own admission, and the other transferable to ladies, or to gentlemen residing six miles distant. So great is the number of applications for admission as members, that as many as three hundred names are usually on the books; and persons have frequently to wait three years and upwards before their chance by rotation arrives, the members being limited in number. To gratify the critical taste of Manchester, which is admitted to be of a high order, the first talent is always engaged. The orchestra consists of upwards of sixty performers. Admittance to the concerts is not purchaseable, and no person can enter except by a subscriber's ticket.*

He adds that there are no 'fixed evenings of performance, concerts being regulated by the availability of English or Foreign professional talent'.[32]

In 1831 the society opened the Concert Hall in Lower Mosley Street, in the centre of Manchester, on part of the site now occupied by the Midland Hotel, and diagonally opposite St Peter's Church, built by James Wyatt in 1788–94, but demolished in 1907.[33] Nearby was Barry's Royal Institution, now part of Manchester Art Gallery [plate 11]. The Concert Hall (later known as the Gentlemen's Concert Hall) was designed by Richard Lane (1795–1880), the leading Manchester

THE ROYAL INSTITUTION, MANCHESTER.

[Plate 11] Royal Institution, Mosley Street, Manchester (1824–35),
by Charles Barry, now part of Manchester Art Gallery, with St Peter's Church to
the right, diagonally opposite the site of the Gentlemen's Concert Hall
Drawn by John Harwood, engraved by Richard Winkles, 1829

architect practising in the Greek revival style during the 1820s and
1830s, whose distinguished public buildings in the city included the
Friends' Meeting House (1828–31), and Manchester Corn Exchange
(1836).[34] The Concert Hall consisted of a rectangular block with an
entrance portico of six unfluted Corinthian columns, leading into a
square entrance hall with stairs giving access to the auditorium on the
first floor; the outer bays of the entrance façade, framed by engaged
columns, flanked a recessed central section [plates 12, 13, 14]. With its
high modelling, and allusions to Stuart and Revett's *The Antiquities
of Athens* (1762), notes Clare Hartwell, it looks as if Lane 'selected
several appropriate motifs and brought them together in a striking
and original composition'.[35]

As the building was demolished in 1897–8, we can do no more than
imagine its interior. In 1842, Love remarked that 'the internal arrange-
ments are fitted up with a splendour which is in accordance with the
musical spirit for which Manchester is celebrated'. He continued:
'This concert room, for elegance of design and superb appearance,

[Plate 12] Gentlemen's Concert Hall, Peter Street, Manchester
Detail of pen, ink and water-colour drawing of exterior
Office of Richard Lane, architect, 1831
Manchester City Galleries

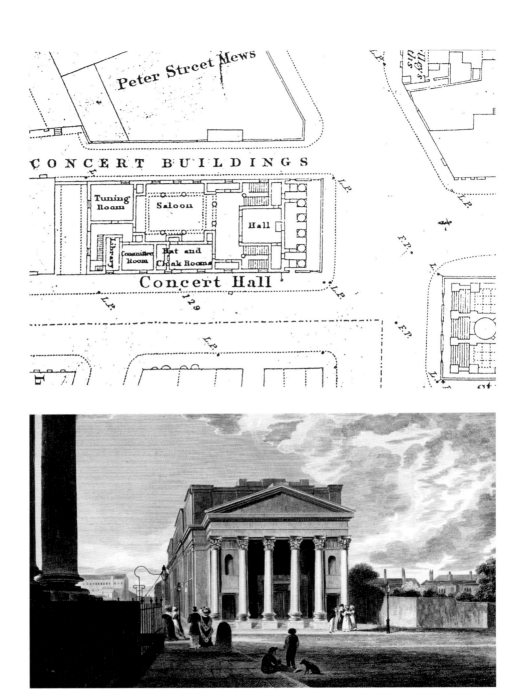

[Plate 13] Gentlemen's Concert Hall, between Peter Street and Mosley Street, Manchester, with St Peter's Church to the right
Ground floor plan, from Ordnance Survey, 5 feet to 1 mile, *c.*1849–51 (sheet 33)

[Plate 14] Gentlemen's Concert Hall, Peter Street, Manchester, with portico of St Peter's Church to the left
Published by T. Sowler, engraved by John Fothergill, 1832

may vie with any in Europe, and presents, on full dress evenings, a brilliant sense of Manchester and its environs; whilst the performances, generally, for correctness of execution, are acknowledged to be unsurpassed by any out of the metropolis.'[36] There is some ambiguity about the date of changes subsequently made internally. A leaflet of 1852, describing the hall, notes that 'on the advice of the architect Mr J. White, the decoration was changed from severe Greek into chaste Italian'.[37] We cannot tell if this was before or after Chopin's concert, but a view from Shaw's *Manchester Old and New,* published in 1896, gives an impression of the interior of the hall a few years before its demolition [plate 15]. As Hallé wrote: 'Few towns are in possession of such a beautiful hall, one in which music can be thoroughly and socially enjoyed.'

Other pianists who had performed in Manchester included John Field, who gave two concerts there in July 1832, for which he was paid 50 guineas, 'certainly the largest fee he received during the whole of his visit to England'.[38] Franz Liszt played in the Theatre Royal as a boy prodigy in 1824 and 1825, visiting the city with his father. He returned in 1840 and gave two concerts, the second on a Broadwood in the Athenaeum; his own Érard, which travelled with him, was already on its way to Ireland.[39] By this time, the Athenaeum, promoting adult education, was the occupant of Manchester's first 'palazzo' building, designed by Charles Barry, not dissimilar in its Italian derivation to Barry's later Reform Club, in London's Pall Mall.[40]

[Plate 15]
Gentlemen's Concert Hall, Peter Street, Manchester
Interior from Willliam Arthur Shaw, *Manchester Old and New …*
(London, [1896]), iii, 36

[Plate 16] Johanna Maria (Jenny) Lind (1820–87), and Marietta Alboni,
Countess Pepoli (*née* Maria Anna Marzia) (1826–94)
Hand-coloured, half-plate daguerreotype, by William Edward Kilburn, 1848

News of Chopin's forthcoming performance in Manchester appears in an advertisement in the *Manchester Guardian* on 9 August 1848, in which the Directors of the Concert Hall

> beg to announce to the Subscribers, that a DRESS CONCERT has been fixed for Monday the 28th of August next, for which the following Performers have been engaged: – Signora ALBONI, Signora CORBARI, Signor SALVI, and Mons. CHOPIN.[41]

The concert was held at 7 pm and, as can be seen, the three singers were all Italian – the contralto Marietta Alboni, Amalia Corbari, '*seconda donna*', and the tenor Lorenzo Salvi. The leader of the orchestra was the Edinburgh-born violinist Charles Alexander Seymour (1810–75), who was active in Manchester musical circles at that time.[42] Alboni (1826–94), regarded as the most celebrated of the artists at the Manchester concert [plate 16], had made her debut at Bologna in 1842 as Clymene in Pacini's *Saffo,* appeared at La Scala the same year, in Vienna in 1843, and spent the winter of 1844–5 in St Petersburg with Tamburini and Pauline Viardot.[43] During the next two years she toured Germany and eastern Europe, making a triumphant London debut on 6 April 1847 as Arsace in Rossini's *Semiramide* to open the first season of the Royal Italian Opera in Covent Garden, where Corbari and Salvi also sang that year. Later in 1847, Alboni made her Parisian debut at the Théâtre Italien, again singing Arsace and also the title role in *La Cenerentola.* In 1848 she returned to Covent Garden to sing Urbain in *Les Huguenots.*[44] Alboni's performance in Manchester was part of a concert tour of the Italian singers arranged by the impresario and composer Thomas Willert Beale;[45] the three performed items from operas by Verdi, Puccini, Rossini, Bellini and Donizetti, and the orchestra played the overtures to Weber's *Der Freischütz,* Beethoven's *Prometheus,* and Rossini's *Il barbiere di Siviglia.*[46]

Despite his commitment to Pleyel when in Paris, Chopin turned to Broadwoods on his visit to Britain.[47] His friendship with the Broadwood family was long-standing, and Henry Fowler Broadwood – son of James Shudi Broadwood, who had entertained him on his visit to London in 1837 – was solicitous of the composer's needs throughout his 1848 stay in England and Scotland; on a practical level, he provided Chopin with pianos for his London lodgings, for some of his metropolitan recitals, and for his concerts in Manchester, Glasgow and Edinburgh.[48] A. J. Hipkins, the English writer on music and musical instruments, was apprenticed to Broadwoods' as a piano tuner

[Plate 17] Broadwood Patent Repetition Grand Pianoforte No. 17047 (London, 1847), played by Chopin in 1848 at London recitals and his Manchester concert
Royal Academy of Music, on permanent loan to the Cobbe Collection Trust, Hatchlands, Surrey

at the age of fourteen and has left significant records on Chopin's habits when in England – describing, for instance, how he went to the Broadwoods' premises with Jane Stirling and carefully chose his pianos.[49] The instrument played by Chopin in Manchester was the Broadwood Patent Repetition Grand Pianoforte No. 17047 (London, 1847), which has a rosewood case, veneered on laminated oak, and is now owned by the Royal Academy of Music, on permanent loan to the Cobbe Collection Trust, Hatchlands, Surrey [plate 17].[50] Chopin had already used this piano for his London recitals at Mrs Sartoris' and the Earl of Falmouth's, and was to play it again at Guildhall on 16 November.[51] As Alec Cobbe's research has revealed, this or other

Broadwood pianos were also employed by Chopin at private engagements at other houses in London.[52]

The identity of the works played by Chopin in his concerts in Britain has long been a matter of debate. Invitations and advertisements give no more than a general impression of intent. This is hardly surprising, in view of his well-known reluctance to perform in public and his difficulties in deciding what to play. Often as not, the final decision was left until the last minute. Chopin's three public concerts outside London – in Manchester, Glasgow and Edinburgh – were all affected in this way.[53] His concert in Manchester was divided into two parts; he performed once in the first part and once in the second [plate 18]. On the day of the concert, a 'notice' issued by the Directors of the Gentlemen's Concert Society indicated that Chopin's advertised programme had been superseded [plate 19], although all the pieces were still his own compositions:

> Part First: Nocturne et Berceuse
> Part Second: Mazourka, Ballade, et Valse

which was changed to

> First Part: Andante and Scherzo
> Second Part: Nocturne, Études, et Berceuse

As part of Willert Beale's 'troupe', the Irish musician George Osborne [plate 20] regularly provided piano accompaniment for the singers, and he did so on this occasion, the *Manchester Guardian* reporting on 30 August that 'Several of the vocal pieces were accompanied by Mr. Osborne, an able composer and pianist.'[54]

What of the reception of the event?[55] The *Manchester Guardian*, again on 30 August, notes that the concert

> *was the most brilliant and interesting which the directors have*
> *given during the season; and there was a larger audience than*
> *we remember to have seen here since the celebrated Grisi and*
> *Alboni concert in September last. Of course, the lustrous-eyed and*
> *liquid-voiced Alboni was the chief attraction of the concert.*

To some members of the audience, however, Chopin was of as much, if not more, interest as Marietta Alboni, for 'he was preceded by a high musical reputation'. His physical appearance, the *Manchester Guardian* noted, was striking:

> *He is very spare in frame, and there is an almost painful air*
> *of feebleness in his appearance and gait. This vanishes when he*

CONCERT HALL, MANCHESTER.

MONDAY EVENING, AUGUST TWENTY-EIGHTH, 1848.

DRESS CONCERT.

MISCELLANEOUS.

Part First.

OVERTURE.............................."Ruler of Spirits"..................................Weber.

TERZETTINO......Signora ALBONI, Signora CORBARI, and Signor SALVI......"Io t'amava"......(Nabuco)......Verdi

RECIT. è CAVATINA......Signora CORBARI......"Come provar"......(La Cantatrice Villane).......Pacini.

ROMANZA..........Signor SALVI.........."Ciel pietoso ".........(Uberto).........Verdi.

NOCTURNE et BERCEUSE—PIANO-FORTE..................Mons. CHOPIN..................Chopin.

CAVATINA è FINALE............Signora ALBONI.........."Non più mesta"..........(Cenerentola)..........Rossini

DUETTO......Signora CORBARI and Signor SALVI......"Vieni in Roma"......(Norma)......Bellini.

An Interval of Twenty Minutes.

It is particularly requested that Parties in promenading round the Hall will keep to the right.

Part Second.

OVERTURE ...."Prometheus"...................................Beethoven.

DUETTO...............Signora ALBONI and Signora CORBARI..............."La Regatta Veneziano "............Rossini

ROMANZA..........Signor SALVI.........."Una furtiva lagrima".........(L'Elisir d'Amore).........Donizetti.

MAZOURKA, BALLADE, et VALSE—PIANO-FORTE.........Mons. CHOPIN.........Chopin.

DUETTO..........Signora ALBONI and Signor SALVI........."Un soave non so che ".......(Cenerentola).........Rossini

ARIA...........Signora CORBARI.........."Oh, dischiuso ".........(Nino).........Verdi.

TYROLIENNE............Signora ALBONI..............."In questo semplice ".............(Betly)............Donizetti

TRIO...Signora ALBONI, Signora CORBARI, and Signor SALVI..."Cruda sorte"...(Ricciardo è Zoraide)...Rossini.

OVERTURE.................."Il Barbiere di Siviglia"..................Rossini.

Leader of the Orchestra..Mr. SEYMOUR.

TO COMMENCE AT SEVEN O'CLOCK PRECISELY.

☞ *The Committee earnestly request the co-operation of the Subscribers in maintaining silence during the Performances*

Subscribers are informed that the 15th Rule will be strictly enforced :—" That no gentleman residing in or within six miles of Manchester is considered as a stranger, or admissible to either Public or Private Concerts without being previously elected a Subscriber ; and that gentlemen who have permanent places of business in Manchester are considered as residents."

No Gentleman will be admitted except in Evening Dress, with either White or Black Cravat.

Carriages, in setting down and taking up Company, are to have their horses' heads towards Oxford-street.

Cave and Sever, Printers, 18, St. Ann's-street, Manchester.

NOTICE.

The Directors beg to inform the Subscribers that Mons. CHOPIN will substitute the following pieces for those inserted in the Programme, viz :—

In the First Part,

ANDANTE and SCHERZO ....Chopin.

In the Second Part,

NOCTURNE, ETUDES, et BERCEUSE ....Chopin.

CONCERT HALL,
August 28th, 1848.

[Plate 18] Programme for Dress Concert, Gentlemen's Concert Hall, Peter Street, Manchester, Monday 28 August 1848
Henry Watson Music Library, Manchester, R780.69 Me68

[Plate 19] Notice of substitutions by Chopin in the programme of the Manchester concert
Henry Watson Music Library, Manchester, R780.69 Me68

G. A. Osborne.

A. Devéria, del.   à Paris, chez Maurice Schlosinger rue Richelieu, 97.   Lith. de C. Motte.

*seats himself at the instrument, in which he seems for the time
perfectly absorbed. Chopin's music and his style of performance
partake of the same leading characteristics – refinement
rather than vigour – subtle elaboration rather than simple
comprehensiveness in composition – an elegant, rapid touch,
rather than a firm, nervous grasp of the instrument.*

The salon rather than the concert hall is his appropriate milieu:

*Both his compositions and his playing appear to be the perfection
of chamber music – fit to be associated with the most refined
instrumental quartets and quartet-playing – but wanting
breadth and obviousness of design, and executive power, to be
effective in a large concert hall.*

Nonetheless, the critic continued, Chopin 'was warmly applauded by
many of the most accomplished amateurs in the town, and he received
an encore in his last piece, a compliment thus accorded to each of the
four London artistes who appeared at this concert'.[56]

The *Manchester Courier and Lancashire General Advertiser* on
30 August praised Chopin's 'chasteness and purity of style' and his
'delicate sensibility of expression', and observed that the concert hall
'was filled to overflowing by a most brilliant audience'.[57] The *Musical
World* (presumably its editor, J. W. Davison) was not so completely
won over. Chopin, it averred, in an article on 9 September,

*certainly played with great finish – too much so, perhaps, and
might have deserved the name of finesse rather – and his delicacy
and expression are unmistakeable; but I missed the astonishing
power of Leopold de Meyer, the vigour of Thalberg, the dash of
Herz, or the grace of Sterndale Bennett.*

Nonetheless, the review concluded, Chopin 'is assuredly a great
pianist, and no one can hear him without receiving some amount of
delectation'.[58]

The critic in the *Manchester Examiner* was able to obtain a ticket
for the concert only 'with the greatest difficulty ... so great was the
desire to hear Alboni'. His impressions of Chopin were mixed: he
'does not quite come up to our idea of a first-rate pianist; it is true
he plays very difficult music (provoking one almost to say with Dr
Johnson, "would that it were impossible!") with beautiful delicacy and

[Plate 20] George Alexander Osborne (1806–93)
Undated lithograph by Charles Motte, from drawing by Achille Devéria

precision of finger but there is no melody or meaning in it'. Chopin's habit of playing only his own work did not always endear him to his audiences, and the *Manchester Examiner*'s writer was not alone in finding Chopin's compositions unappealing. Rather than play one of Beethoven's sonatas, he observed,

> *it is a pity that performers of his ability think it incumbent*
> *on them to astonish rather than please their audiences with*
> *concertos written by themselves, apparently for the express*
> *purpose of cramming into them elaborate passages, chromatiques*
> *and next-to-impossible cadenzas, all of which have no beauty*
> *in themselves, but should only be sparingly used to relieve what*
> *would be otherwise, perhaps, too monotonous a concord of sweet*
> *sounds.*

One wonders what this critic would have thought of Liszt![59]

George Osborne and Chopin were already friends from Paris, where Osborne had lived from 1831 to 1843 and been a pupil of Fétis, Pixis and Kalkbrenner, as well as a teacher of Hallé.[60] A friend of Berlioz as well as of Chopin, Osborne had drawn fashionable audiences to his Parisian concerts, had accompanied Chopin in a performance of his F minor piano concerto in 1832, and in the same year been one of six pianists (including Chopin) who performed together in the *Salons Pleyel*.[61] In 1843 he returned to England, where he played, taught, and composed chamber and violin music, overtures, and two operas. He made frequent trips back to Paris, where his patrons were drawn from the aristocracy and intellectual society, including in particular wealthy Irishmen and Englishmen living in France.[62]

In 1880 Osborne presented a lecture to the Musical Association in London, entitled 'Reminiscences of Fredrick [*sic*] Chopin', which provides us with a fascinating glimpse of Chopin's life in Paris in the 1830s and 1840s; the previous year, Osborne had given the Association a paper on Berlioz. Now he offered his views on Chopin as musician and as personal friend. He explains that, on tour with Alboni in 1848, he

> *met Chopin at Manchester, where he was announced to play*
> *at a grand concert without orchestra. He begged I should not be*
> *present. 'You, my dear Osborne', said he, 'who have heard me*
> *so often in Paris, remain with those impressions. My playing*
> *will be lost in such a large room, and my compositions will be*
> *ineffective. Your presence at the concert will be painful both*
> *to you and me.'*

Despite Chopin's entreaty, Osborne – apart from accompanying Alboni, Corbari and Salvi, at the piano – made a point of listening to Chopin play:

> *I was present, unknown to him, in a remote corner of the room, where I helped to cheer and applaud him. I heard him then for the last time, when his prediction was fulfilled in part, for his playing was too delicate to create enthusiasm, and I felt truly sorry for him.*

Having said this, Osborne adds, Chopin's 'performance at that concert, however, has not effaced those pleasurable and vivid emotions which I hope ever to retain of his playing and of himself'.[63]

On 4 August 1848 Hermann Léo – brother of Auguste Léo, whose salon Chopin frequented in Paris – wrote to Charles Hallé, inviting him to come to Manchester,[64] and it is probable, but not certain, that Hallé was present at Chopin's concert there later that month. Hallé, too, was a supporter of Broadwoods. In his *Autobiography*, he records that in the summer, not long after his arrival, he attended a concert of the Gentlemen's Concert Society, at which

> *Grisi, Mario, and Lablache sang; but the orchestra! oh, the orchestra! I was fresh from the 'Concerts du Conservatoire', from Hector Berlioz' orchestra, and I seriously thought of packing up and leaving Manchester, so that I might not have to endure a second of these wretched performances.[65]*

On the other hand, elsewhere in his *Autobiography*, Hallé writes: 'I had the pleasure ... to welcome [Chopin] to Manchester, where he played at one of the concerts of the society called the Gentlemen's Concerts in the month of August. It was then painfully evident that his end was drawing near; a year later he was no more.' What did Hallé mean by 'welcoming' Chopin? Did they meet when Chopin was staying with the Schwabes? If Hallé attended Chopin's Manchester concert, he would surely have specifically said so.[66]

One puzzle remains about Chopin's visit to Manchester: Did he perform twice? If he did so, the most likely location for a private recital was Crumpsall House. Jenny Lind had sung there, and it is well known that Chopin entertained his hosts when staying at Scottish country seats. At Crumpsall, says Susanna Brookshaw, Chopin

> *was in congenial surroundings amongst people he liked, and what was often done from a sense of duty or obligation, would, one feels sure, be done as a pleasure in this instance, if only to*

recall happier days in Paris, when he and his friends met for music at Léo's house. There must have been a piano provided for his use in his own room or elsewhere, in order that he might prepare for the concert.

To Brookshaw, 'the belief that he played at Crumpsall House grows to absolute certainty', and she urges us to 'let the mind's eye dwell for a moment upon a picture of Chopin playing after dinner in the drawing-room'.[67] Perhaps it was on such an occasion at Crumpsall that a curious happening occurred.

In 1974, in his book *Frédéric Chopin*, Bernard Gavoty noted that on 29 August, the day after his concert in the Gentlemen's Concert Hall, Chopin performed his Sonata in B flat minor (op. 35) in a salon in Manchester. Having played the allegro and scherzo, Chopin 'left the room, coming back to the audience a few minutes later to play the march and finale, without pause. The next day, the critic of the *Manchester Guardian*, who had been invited as a friend, wrote in astonishment at this brief interruption.'[68] Was he ill? Chopin was asked on the spot. The answer, Gavoty claimed, lay in a letter from Chopin to Solange Clésinger of 9 September 1848. In this letter, which Gavoty owned, Chopin wrote:

> *A strange thing happened to me while I was playing my Sonata in B-flat Minor for some British friends. I had played the allegro and the scherzo successfully, and I was going to attack the march when, suddenly, I saw the cursed creatures that one lugubrious night appeared to me at the monastery rising from the case of the piano. I had to go out for a moment to collect myself, after which I resumed playing without saying a word to anyone.*

Gavoty commented: 'Chopin did not talk about his music; after he created it, he lived it.'[69] Is it significant that the third of the four movements of this sonata is known as the Funeral March?[70]

A. J. (SANDY) SCOTT

After Chopin's return to Scotland, those who provide us with further links to Manchester include Salis and Julie Schwabe, and Sandy Scott [plate 21]. From 1851 to 1857, Alexander John Scott was the first principal of Owens College, later the University of Manchester.[71] The Schwabes were also friends of both Scott and Thomas Erskine, of Linlathen, a cousin of Jane Stirling; in 1847, before he moved to Manchester, Scott had given lectures to Salis Schwabe's employees at his factory at Rhodes.[72] Scott was born in 1805, the son of a minister of the Church of Scotland. He graduated MA at the University of Glasgow in 1824, and was licensed by the presbytery of Paisley. As J. Philip Newell explains, 'within months of his licensing Scott began to express doubt concerning the traditional Calvinism of the Scottish church, specifically its doctrine of the love of God being limited to the elect'. He became tutor to the family of Thomas Erskine, of Linlathen, who had recently published two books, *Remarks on the Internal Evidence for the Truth of Revealed Religion* (1820) and *An Essay on Faith* (1822). Scott was in sympathy with both works, and subsequently he and Erskine became lifelong friends.[73] In 1828, Scott joined Edward Irving in London, and 'developed a theology that appealed to the authority of the spiritual conscience, an inner faculty capable of discerning spiritual truth'. In 1831, he was deposed from the ministry, but for the next fifteen years used the tiny Woolwich Chapel as his base for teaching and preaching.[74]

When working at Woolwich, from 1831 to 1846, Scott travelled to the Continent, notably to Switzerland and France, and it was during these years that he seems to have met both Ary Scheffer and Chopin; indeed, it has been suggested that Scott may have been assembling material for a biography of the composer. Clearly Jane Stirling, as a relative and close friend of Thomas Erskine, of Linlathen, would

[PLATE 21] The Revd Alexander John (Sandy) Scott (1805–66)
Portrait from John Hair, *Regent Square: Eighty Years of a London Congregation*, rev. ed. (London, 1899), opposite p.86

[Plate 22] Chopin: plaster death mask,
based on original by Auguste Clésinger, Paris, 1849
Gift of Miss Susan Fisher Scott to the Royal Manchester
College of Music, 1910

[Plate 23] Chopin: plaster left hand, based on original by Auguste Clésinger,
Paris, 1849
Gift of Miss Susan Fisher Scott to the Royal Manchester
College of Music, 1910

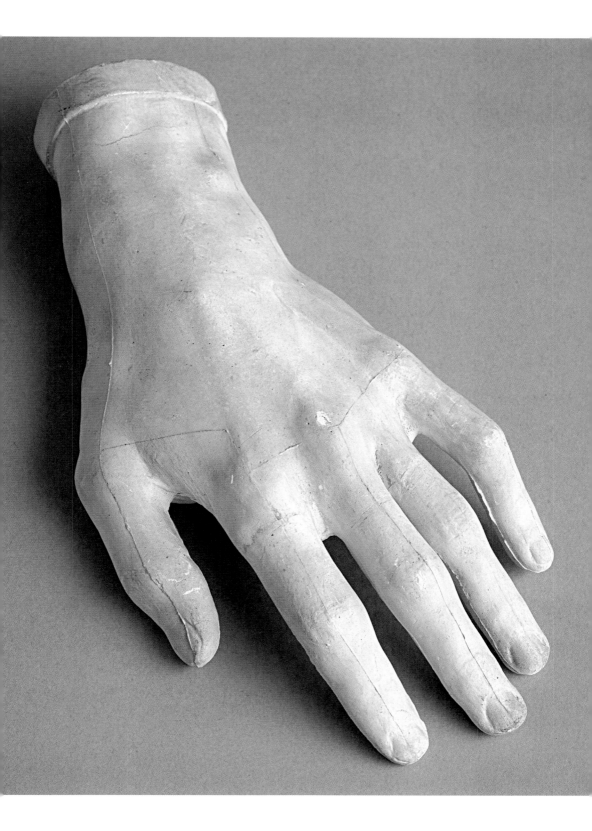

have been able to offer him significant help. In 1910, Scott's daughter, Miss Susan Fisher Scott, presented plaster casts of Chopin's death mask and of his left hand to the Royal Manchester College of Music [plates 22, 23], and it is not impossible that both of these were given to Sandy Scott by Jane Stirling.[75] The sculptor was Auguste Clésinger, who had married Solange Dudevant-Sand, daughter of George Sand, in 1847, and whose work included a bust of Sand (1847) and Chopin's head on the composer's grave in the Père Lachaise cemetery in Paris (1850). In 1973, the Frederick Chopin Society of Poland presented the Royal Northern College of Music with a full-length bronze statue of Chopin by the Polish sculptor Ludwika Nitschowa to mark the 125th anniversary of Chopin's concert in Manchester in 1848 [plate 24].[76]

Salis Schwabe died at Glyn Garth on 23 July 1853, at the age of fifty-three.[77] After her husband's death, Mrs Julie Schwabe continued to entertain at her Welsh home. In 1857, the year of the Manchester Exhibition of Art Treasures, visitors included Ary Scheffer, who stayed first at Crumpsall House for three weeks and then at Glyn Garth. Here, wrote Mrs Grote, 'were present, in ample store, all those elements in which an imaginative, sentimental, and affectionate soul, like that of Scheffer, might find delectation and refreshment', including 'the picturesque mountain scenery of Carnarvonshire, the sight of the shipping gliding about in the "Menai"; [and] the novel spectacle of the Welsh people, busy, yet not toil-worn'.[78]

CHOPIN'S RETURN TO PARIS

After returning to Scotland from Manchester early in September 1848, Chopin continued his travels around Scottish country seats, and gave concerts in the Merchants' Hall, Glasgow, on Wednesday 27 September, and in the Hopetoun Rooms, Edinburgh, on Wednesday 4 October.[79] In Glasgow he appeared with the singer Madame Giulietta Adelasio de Marguerittes, but in Edinburgh he was the sole performer. From two surviving programmes, it seems that the pieces he played in both concerts were not dissimilar – a mixture of ballades, études, impromptus, mazurkas, nocturnes, preludes and waltzes, and the berceuse. On 31 October Chopin took the train from Edinburgh to London, and on Thursday 16 November gave the final public performance of his career as part of the Annual Grand Dress and Fancy Ball and Concert in aid of the Literary Association of the Friends of Poland. A week later, on Thursday 23 November, Chopin left London for Paris, arriving there the next day.

Once back in Paris, Chopin's health was, of course, a major concern. Among the many visitors who came to see him were friends from England and Scotland, including Jane Stirling, Mrs Erskine and Princess Marcelina Czartoryska. Henry Fowler Broadwood was invited to Paris by the composer, but nothing came of it. From Manchester, the Schwabes and the Léos must surely have been attentive, too. Chopin died on 17 October 1849, and his funeral service was held in the Madeleine ten days later. Teofil Kwiatowski made death-bed sketches, and Auguste Clésinger provided death masks (a version of which was to end up in Manchester), and set to work on his sculptured head to be set in the Chopin monument in the Père Lachaise cemetery the next year. Writing to Mrs Grote from the United States, after Chopin's death, Jenny Lind observed mournfully of her own last visit to Paris: 'Poor dear Chopin, he was not there.'[80]

[Plate 24] Chopin: bronze statue by Ludwika Nitschowa (1889–1989) Gift of Frederick Chopin Society of Poland to the Royal Northern College of Music, Manchester, 1973, to mark the 125th anniversary of Chopin's concert in the city in 1848

ACKNOWLEDGEMENTS

In addition to acknowledgements made in the preface and notes, I should like to thank Karen Andrews, Robert Evans, Penny Icke, Angharad Jones, Thomas Lloyd, Camwy MacDonald, Stella Schultz, Gwilym Tawy, Anne Venables and Elisabeth Whittle, for information on Glyn Garth; John H. G. Archer and Clare Hartwell, for advice on the history of Manchester architecture in general, and the Gentlemen's Concert Hall in particular; Rose Cholmondeley and Alec Cobbe, for observations on the Broadwoods; Paul Collen and Oliver Davies, for help with portraits; Rosemary Firman and Una Hunt, for material on George Osborne; J. Philip Newell, for guidance on A. J. Scott; David Taylor, formerly of Manchester Central Library, for aid with the documentation of Manchester's history, and Paul Muir Wood, for assistance with research on John Muir Wood and his family. For editorial help I am grateful to James Albisetti, John H. G. Archer, David Fallows and Martin Thacker.

NOTES & REFERENCES

1. *Chopin in Manchester* incorporates material from my PhD thesis, 'Chopin in Britain: Chopin's Visits to England and Scotland in 1837 and 1848. People, Places, and Activities' (Durham University, 2009), prepared under the direction of Jeremy Dibble, to whom I am greatly indebted.

2. For accessible summaries in English of Chopin's life and work, see the entry on 'Fryderyk Franciscek Chopin' by Kornel Michałowski and Jim Samson in *Oxford Music Online*, and the website of The Fryderyk Chopin Institute, Warsaw (http://en.chopin.nifc.pl/ chopin). For the Chopin literature, see William Smialek and Maja Trochimczyk, *Frédéric Chopin: A Research and Information Guide*, Routledge Music Bibliographies, 2nd edn. (Abingdon, 2011).

3. Ferdinand Hiller, trans. M. E. von Glehn, *Mendelssohn: Letters and Recollections* (London, 1874; repr. 1972), 101.

4. [Ignaz Moscheles], *Recent Music and Musicians …* (New York, 1873; repr. 1970), 240.

5. William Stirling (1818–78) became Sir William Stirling Maxwell, 9th Bt, on succeeding to the baronetcy in 1865. In 1847, on the death of his father, he inherited Keir House, Perthshire, and entertained Chopin there in 1848. That same year, he published his three-volume *Annals of the Artists of Spain*, which had been preceded in 1847 by an accompanying volume of Talbotype illustrations. The list of domestic settings in which Chopin may have played in London is constantly being added to. See, e.g., those considered in Alec Cobbe, *Chopin's Swansong: The Paris and London Pianos of His Last Performances Now in the Cobbe Collection* (London, 2010).

6. Susanna Brookshaw, *Concerning Chopin in Manchester* (Manchester, 1937; repr., with additional information, 1951); and Susanna Brookshaw, 'Concerning Chopin in Manchester', *Hinrichsen's Musical Year Book*, 4–5 (1947–8),

189–91. See also Brookshaw's article 'Chopin's Jane Stirling', *Musical Opinion* (April 1948), 254–5, reprinted in *Concerning Chopin in Manchester*, 38–40.

7. Arthur Hedley, *Selected Correspondence of Fryderyk Chopin* (London, 1962; repr. 1979), 339. Peter Thorpe, of the National Railway Museum, York, informs me that the rail journey from Edinburgh to Manchester may have lasted longer than this.

8. See Jack Simmons and Gordon Biddle, *The Oxford Companion to British Railway History, from 1603 to the 1990s* (Oxford, 1997), 65–6, 284–6, 308–10. The case for Salford Station is made by Brookshaw, *Concerning Chopin in Manchester*, 31–2. The identification of London Road Station, Manchester, and the names of the railway companies, I owe to Peter Thorpe. Caledonian Railway trains departed from Lothian Street Station, Edinburgh, which had opened in February 1848.

9. For Manchester's vigorous intellectual and social life during this period, see, e.g., Howard Michael Wach's two articles, 'Culture and the Middle Classes: Popular Knowledge in Industrial Manchester', *The Journal of British Studies*, 27/4 (1988), 375–404; and 'A "Still, Small Voice" from the Pulpit: Religion and the Creation of Social Morality in Manchester, 1820–50', *The Journal of Modern History*, 63/3 (1991), 425–56. See also John H. G. Archer, ed., *Art and Architecture in Victorian Manchester: Ten Illustrations of Patronage and Practice* (Manchester, 1985).

10. Hedley, *Chopin Correspondence*, 339. 'Mrs Rich' was Mary Rich (*née* Mackintosh) (1789–1876), who in 1808 married Claudius James Rich (1786/7–1821), traveller and collector of manuscripts and antiquities. She was aunt of Fanny Erskine.

11. For the Schwabes, see James C. Albisetti, 'The "Inevitable Schwabes": An Introduction', *Transactions of the Lancashire and Cheshire Antiquarian Society*, 98 (2002), 91–112. James Albisetti, whose dual biography of Salis and Julie Schwabe is in preparation, gave invaluable assistance with my research on the Schwabes. See also the articles in the *Oxford DNB Online* on Salis Schwabe, by Patrick Waddington, and on Julie Schwabe, by Bill Williams.

12. Crumpsall House is shown in Brookshaw, *Concerning Chopin in Manchester*, frontispiece, and the plates between pp.32–3.

13. William Edward Armitage Axon, ed., *The Annals of Manchester: A Chronological Record from the Earliest Times to the End of 1885* (Manchester and London, 1886), 241.

14. Axon, *Annals of Manchester*, 247. The context of Lind's performances in Manchester can be seen in Robert Beale, 'Opera in Manchester, 1848–1899', *Manchester Sounds*, 6 (2005–6), 71–97, at p.84. An autograph notebook, in Swedish, recording Lind's operatic performances, including those in the English provinces in 1847–9, was sold in Sotheby's sale of Musical Manuscripts, London, 19 May 2006 (lot 92).

15. The bust of Salis Schwabe by Bally is now in the care of the Middleton Civic Association at the Old Grammar School, Middleton. For Bally, see Ingrid Roscoe, Emma Hardy and M. G. Sullivan, *A Biographical Dictionary of Sculptors in Britain, 1660–1851* (New Haven and London, 2009), 65. The Schwabe bust, however, is not mentioned here in the entry on Bally. It was presented to the Middleton Civic Association in 1993 by A. Brunnschweiler & Co. Ltd, Manchester, through the kind offices of Carl Goldberg, and I am grateful to Morris Garratt and Alan Seabright for arranging access and photography.

16. I thank Peter Weston for enabling me to see the painting of Mrs Schwabe by Scheffer at Roehampton University, and for providing a photograph of it.

17. For the Schwabes and Scheffer, see Edward Morris, 'Ary Scheffer and his English Circle', *Oud Holland*, 99/4 (1985), 294–323.

18. Thomas Dyke Acland Tellefsen (1825–74), the Norwegian pianist, teacher and composer, was a pupil of Chopin in Paris from 1844 to 1846. For his friendship with the Schwabes, and their circle, see Jeremy Barlow, 'Encounters with Chopin: Fanny Erskine's Paris Diary, 1847–1848', in John Rink and Jim Samson, eds., *Chopin Studies 2* (Cambridge, 1994), 245–8.

19. Hedley, *Chopin Correspondence*, 340. James Albisetti tells me that an entry for 7 December 1847, in a transcript of Fanny Erskine's diary, notes that she and Mrs Rich dined at the Parisian home of Jane Stirling's sister, Mrs Katherine Erskine, 'and the only other company Chopin'.

20. In a letter to Gryzmała, at the end of July 1848, Chopin writes in the past tense of Neukomm living with the Schwabes, but tells his family in Warsaw, in a letter of 10–19 August 1848, that Neukomm was then 'staying with' them. See Hedley, *Chopin Correspondence*, 326, 339. James Albisetti adds that Neukomm underwent surgery at Manchester Eye Hospital, and that Geraldine Jewsbury's letters to Jane Welsh Carlyle describe how she read to him at Crumpsall House.

21. Details of versions of 'Wiosna' (published posthumously as op. 74, no. 2), are in Krystyna Kobylańska, *Rękopisy utworów Chopina: Katalog / Manuscripts of Chopin's Works: Catalogue*, 2 vols. (Warsaw, 1981), i, 434–40 (nos. 1101–12).

22. Hedley, *Chopin Correspondence*, 340–2.

23. Roger Redfern, *Guardian*, Tuesday 8 June 2010, Country Diary, 30.

24. The design of Glyn Garth is attributed to Gregan in *The Dictionary of Architecture, Issued by the Architectural Publication Society*, iii [1864], 86, which also lists a house in Victoria Park, Manchester, for 'Mr. J. M. Schwabe'. For Gregan, see the article on him in the *Oxford DNB Online* by C. W. Sutton, revised by Valerie Scott.

25. For Glyn Garth (otherwise Glyn-y-Garth), see Thomas Lloyd, *The Lost Houses of Wales: A Survey of Country Houses in Wales Demolished Since c.1900*, 2nd edn. (London, 1989), 16, 118. Albisetti, 'The "Inevitable Schwabes"', 94, notes that the Schwabes purchased Glyn Garth from Hugh Beever in 1850, and cites as his source the *Manchester Courier*, 30 July 1853, 7. Glyn Garth was sold by the Schwabe family in 1898. A set of magnificent photographs of the interior of Glyn Garth, taken by Walter Scott in 1948, is held by the National Monuments Record of Wales, Aberystwyth.

26. Peter Weston, *The Froebel Educational Institute: The Origins and History of the College* (Roehampton, 2002), 4–5.

27. Winifred Gérin, *Elizabeth Gaskell: A Biography* (Oxford, 1981), 145. For Mrs Gaskell's correspondence with the Schwabes, see J. A. V. Chapple and Arthur Pollard, eds., *The Letters of Mrs Gaskell*, 2nd edn. (Manchester, [1997]), nos. 113, 121, 122, 128, 162. See also Jenny Uglow, *Elizabeth Gaskell: A Habit of Stories*, new edn. (London, 1999), 161, for observations on visitors to Crumpsall House.

28. Rosemary Ashton, *Little Germany: Exile and Asylum in Victorian England* (Oxford, 1996), 207.

29. Morris, 'Ary Scheffer and his English Circle', 307, 306.

30. See Edward Morris, *French Art in Nineteenth-Century Britain* (New Haven and London, 2005), *passim*.

31. Wilfred Allis, 'The Gentlemen's Concerts, Manchester, 1777–1920' (MPhil thesis, University of Manchester, 1995); Rachel Gick, 'Chamber Music Concerts in Manchester, 1838–1844', *Manchester Sounds*, 2 (2001), 59–87; and Rachel Gick, 'Concert Life in Manchester, 1800–1848' (PhD thesis, University of Manchester, 2003). For the Gentlemen's Concert Society, see the Henry Watson Music Library, Manchester Central Library, R780.68 Me68 MIC, containing minutes, 1830–1920; and R780.69 Me68 MIC, containing programmes of the Gentlemen's Concerts, 1840–9.

32. Benjamin Love, *The Hand-Book of Manchester … 2nd edn.* (Manchester, 1842), 274–5.

33. See Clare Hartwell, with contributions by John H. G. Archer and Julian Holder, *Manchester*, Pevsner Architectural Guides (New Haven and London, 2001; repr. 2002), 202–3; and Clare Hartwell, Matthew Hyde and Nikolaus Pevsner, *Lancashire: Manchester and the South-East*, The Buildings of England (New Haven and London, 2004), 332–3.

34. For Lane, see Clare Hartwell, 'Manchester and the Golden Age of Pericles: Richard Lane, Architect', in Clare Hartwell and Terry Wyke, eds., *Making Manchester: Aspects of the History of Architecture in the City and Region since 1800. Essays in Honour of John H. G. Archer* (Manchester, 2007), 18–35; and Clare Hartwell's article on Lane in the *Oxford DNB Online*. Manchester City Libraries (Misc/324) hold three drawings by Alfred Waterhouse, dated 18 January 1861, showing the architect's proposals for alterations to each floor of the Gentlemen's Concert Hall.

35. Hartwell, 'Manchester and the Golden Age of Pericles', 23.

36. Love, *The Hand-Book of Manchester*, 274–5.

37. Allis, 'Gentlemen's Concerts, Manchester, 1777–1920', 51. The subsequent quotation by Hallé is from Hartwell, 'Manchester and the Golden Age of Pericles', 24.

38. Patrick Piggott, *The Life and Music of John Field (1782–1837), Creator of the Nocturne* (London, 1973), 51.

39. William Wright, 'Liszt in Manchester', *Journal of the American Liszt Society*, 41 (1997), 1–20. David Ian Allsobrook, *Liszt: My Travelling Circus Life* (London, 1991), 38, notes that Liszt journeyed 'sometimes by rail, but mainly by coach and horses, with a separate van to carry his precious Érard piano, which could be mounted on a railway wagon whenever necessary'.

40. Hartwell, Hyde and Pevsner, *Lancashire: Manchester and the South-East*, 289–90.

41. *Manchester Guardian*, Wednesday 9 August 1848, 1. An edited version of this appears in Frederick Niecks, *Frederick Chopin as Man and Musician,* 3rd edn., 2 vols. (London, [1902]), ii, 294.

42. For Seymour, see James Brown and Stephen Stratton, *British Musical Biography …* (London, 1897; repr. 1971), 366.

43. This paragraph draws on the entry on Alboni by Elizabeth Forbes in *Oxford Music Online.*

44. Harold Rosenthal, *Two Centuries of Opera at Covent Garden* (London, 1958), 72–84.

45. See the entry on Beale by Michael Musgrave in the *Oxford DNB Online.* The singers, and Osborne, were contracted to Cranmer & Co., and Beale was their 'personal conductor'.

46. This 'provincial tour' of England and Scotland lasted a month, and is described in Thomas Willert Beale (pseud. Walter Maynard), *The Light of Other Days, Seen Through the Wrong End of an Opera Glass,* 2 vols. (London, 1890), i, 95–107.

47. Surrey History Centre (Woking), John Broadwood & Sons, Ltd, piano manufacturers, London. Business records, 1719–1981. I am grateful to Robert Simonson for making these available to me, and for other assistance.

48. Cobbe, *Chopin's Swansong*, 18–27.

49. On Hipkins's authority we know that Chopin played Broadwood Patent Repetition Grand Pianoforte No. 17001 (London, *c.*1847) in his Glasgow and Edinburgh concerts. See Cobbe, *Chopin's Swansong*, 25.

50. Alec Cobbe, *Composer Instruments: A Catalogue of the Cobbe Collection of Keyboard Instruments with Composer Associations* (Hatchlands, 2000), 59–61. The piano is also described and illustrated in Jean-Jacques Eigeldinger, *Chopin et Pleyel* (Paris, 2010), 250–1.

51. Prior to its use at Guildhall, Chopin had the piano at his lodgings at 4 St James's Place.

52. Cobbe, *Chopin's Swansong*, 22–7. 'No. 17047 was sold on 21 September 1849 for 160 guineas to a George Wigg of 61 Westbourne Terrace' (p.27).

53. Chopin's concerts in Scotland were arranged and promoted by John Muir Wood (1805–92), musician, writer, publisher and pioneering photographer. His son Herbert Kemlo Wood (1866–1953) comments on Chopin's Glasgow concert: 'Chopin could not make up his mind about the programme, he preferred to play as the spirit moved him and often changed his mind. This accounts for the lack of Opus numbers on the printed programme. The pieces played are identified only from the manuscript jottings in my father's handwriting on the programme in my possession.' This problem, Herbert Wood explains, applied to Chopin's concerts in both Edinburgh and Glasgow: 'Chopin's habit by this time seemed to have been to put down 'Etudes, Nocturnes, Mazurkas', and so on, and on the day he would play of these what he felt inclined to.' Thus the day before he was due to perform in Edinburgh he wrote to Grzymała in Paris that he still had not 'seen the hall or settled the programme'. At both the Glasgow and Edinburgh concerts, Herbert Wood adds, the audiences 'were almost entirely made up of Chopin's aristocratic friends, principally ladies of whom he always had a devoted following'. Herbert Kemlo Wood, 'Chopin in Britain, 11', *The Voice of Poland*, 2/21 (17 October 1943), 6, 10.

54. *Manchester Guardian*, Wednesday 30 August 1848, 7. An edited version of this appears in William G. Atwood, *Fryderyk Chopin: Pianist from Warsaw* (New York, 1987), 253. An enthusiastic letter, in support of Chopin, was published in the *Manchester Guardian*, 6 September 1848, 7. It was written by the German organologist and musicologist Carl Engel (1818–82), and appears in Brookshaw, *Concerning Chopin in Manchester*, 24–5. On Wednesday 20 September 1848, the front page of the *Manchester Guardian* carried an advertisement by Chopin's London music publishers, Wessel & Co., for 'the inimitable Works of FREDERIC CHOPIN'.

55. Reviews of the concert in the *Manchester Courier* (30 August), the *Manchester Guardian* (30 August), the *Manchester Examiner*

(5 September), and the *Musical World* (9 September), are given (edited, and with some elisions) in Atwood, *Pianist from Warsaw*, 251–3. Another review appears in the *Manchester Times* and *Manchester and Salford Advertiser and Chronicle*, Saturday 2 September 1848, 5.

56. *Manchester Guardian*, Wednesday 30 August 1848, 7. The review ends with a paragraph of criticism of artists who fail to decide on their programmes in good time. Versions of the review appear in Niecks, *Chopin as Man and Musician*, ii, 295, and Atwood, *Pianist from Warsaw*, 253. On pp.245–60, Atwood gives a selection of reviews of Chopin's concerts in London, Manchester, Glasgow and Edinburgh.

57. Niecks, *Chopin as Man and Musician*, ii, 295.

58. Atwood, *Pianist from Warsaw*, 252.

59. Atwood, *Pianist from Warsaw*, 251–2.

60. See the entries on Osborne by R. H. Legge, revised by Rosemary Firman, in the *Oxford DNB Online*, and by Jean Mongrédien's in *Oxford Music Online*.

61. Niecks, *Chopin as Man and Musician*, i, 241.

62. Una Hunt, 'George Alexander Osborne: A Nineteenth-Century Irish Pianist-Composer' (PhD thesis, National University of Ireland, Maynooth, 2006).

63. See George Alexander Osborne, 'Reminiscences of Fredrick [*sic*] Chopin', *Proceedings of the Musical Association*, 6 (1879–80), 91–105, at p.101. As Osborne was speaking and writing over thirty years after the Manchester concert, his memory may have played him false.

64. *Life and Letters of Sir Charles Hallé, Being an Autobiography (1819–1860) with Correspondence and Diaries* (London, 1896), 230.

65. Michael Kennedy, ed., *The Autobiography of Sir Charles Hallé, with Correspondence and Diaries* (London, 1972), 122–3. Brookshaw, *Concerning Chopin in Manchester*, 4, indicates that Jane Stirling and Mrs Katherine Erskine heard Chopin in Manchester. Unfortunately, Brookshaw has misread the letters she quotes on p.10, and this is unlikely.

66. Hallé, *Autobiography*, 56–7. Hallé was urged to stay by his friends, who 'gave [him] to understand that [he] was expected to change all this – to accomplish a revolution, in fact' (p. 123). Which, of course, he duly did.

67. Brookshaw, *Concerning Chopin in Manchester*, 18. Brookshaw likewise speculates on this in 'Concerning Chopin in Manchester', *Hinrichsen's Musical Year Book*, 4–5 (1947–8), 190.

68. See Bernard Gavoty, *Frédéric Chopin* (Paris, 1974; repr. 1986), 298–300, 418n3. The English text here is from Martin Sokolinsky's translation of Gavoty's *Chopin* (New York, 1977), 233. I have been unable to find any references in the *Manchester Guardian* to this possible second recital.

69. Gavoty, *Chopin*, 299, indicates that he bought the letter in London, but its present whereabouts are unknown. The date of 9 September 1848 suggests that the letter, if authentic, was written at Johnstone Castle, Renfrewshire, where Chopin was then staying with the Houstons.

70. I am grateful to Jeffrey Kallberg for alerting me to this incident. For fuller details, see his two articles, 'La *Marche* de Chopin', in Jean-Jacques Eigeldinger and Jacqueline Waeber, eds., *Frédéric Chopin: Interprétations* (Geneva, 2005), 11–42; and 'Chopin's March, Chopin's Death', *Nineteenth-Century Music*, 25/1 (2001), 3–26, at pp.22–3. The authenticity of the letter is considered in n59 of this second article, and in n58 references are given to George Sand's description in her *Oeuvres autobiographiques* of the 'cursed creatures' which Chopin saw in the Carthusian monastery at Valldemossa, Mallorca. Other references to Chopin's ghostly apparitions are in Hedley, *Chopin Correspondence*, 347.

71. J. Philip Newell, *Listening for the Heartbeat of God: A Celtic Spirituality* (London, 1997; repr. 2008), 62–73.

72. On 8 October and 20 October 1847, A. J. Scott gave two lectures at the Mechanics' Institute, Rhodes, 'to the workpeople of Mr. Salis Schwabe', with the titles 'On Education', and 'The Foundations of Society, Moral and

Economical'. See Joseph Thompson, *The Owens College …* (Manchester, 1886), 653.

73. In 1838, Erskine wrote movingly to Jane Stirling on the death of Mme de Broglie, who had translated his writings into French, and in 1859 to Mrs Julie Schwabe, on the death of Jane Stirling. Erskine's letters to Mrs Schwabe, of 1851–68, are in the National Library of Scotland, Edinburgh, MS 9747.

74. The quotations in this paragraph, and the one below, are from Newell's entry on Scott in the *Oxford DNB Online*. From 1848 to 1851, Scott was Professor of English Language and Literature at University College London, and one of the founders of Bedford College, 'the first centre of higher education for women in Britain based on the principles of religious freedom'; the fledgling Owens College, Manchester, to which Scott moved in 1851, was also free of religious tests. Scott continued 'to pursue the development of education for the working classes, and in 1858, along with others, he founded the Manchester Working Men's College', and established connections with the wider artistic, intellectual, political, and socially committed community in Manchester.

75. For assistance with my research at the Royal Northern College of Music I am grateful to the College Librarian, Anna Wright, and the photographer, Michael Pollard. The casts are illustrated and described in William Waterhouse, *Royal Northern College of Music, Collection of Historic Music Instruments: Catalogue of the Collection* (Manchester, 2010), 274–6. There is no mention of the casts in Jane Stirling's will and inventory, National Archives of Scotland (Edinburgh), SC70//4/63, Edinburgh Sheriff Court Wills, and SC70/1/100, Edinburgh Sheriff Court Inventories, respectively. The mask, and Jane Stirling's connection with it, are considered in R. J. Forbes, 'The Death-Mask of Chopin', *Manchester Guardian*, Wednesday 22 February 1933.

76. It is set on a marble base, and is described and illustrated in Terry Wyke, with Harry Cocks, *Public Sculpture of Greater Manchester* (Liverpool, 2004), 49–50. Marita Albán Juárez and Ewa

Sławińsaka Dahlig inform me that there are other casts of Nitschowa's statue in Guadalahara, Mexico, and in the gardens of the Sanniki Palace, Poland.

77. As Axon, *Annals of Manchester*, 264, records: 'Mr Salis Schwabe died at Glyn Garth, on the Menai Straits, July 23 [1853], in his 54th year. He was buried at Harpurhey Cemetery July 30, and was followed to the grave by the Bishop of Manchester and many of the leading persons of the city.'

78. Mrs [Harriet] Grote, *Memoir of the Life of Ary Scheffer* (London, 1860), 115–19.

79. The following paragraph is based on material from my thesis, 'Chopin in Britain', chapters 8–10 and the conclusion.

80. Catalogue of Sotheby's sale of Continental Manuscripts and Music, London, 26 May 1994, p.19 (lot 274 (iv)). Lots 248–81 consisted of a Jenny Lind archive.

CHOPIN IN MANCHESTER

IN AUGUST 1848, towards the end of a seven-month stay in Britain and a little over a year before he died, Chopin made his one and only visit to Manchester.[1] Spurred on by the February Revolution, he had left Paris for London, where he taught and gave recitals, and that summer found himself in Edinburgh. It was from Edinburgh that Chopin took the train to Manchester.

Chopin had arrived in the French capital in 1831, aged twenty-one, having travelled from Warsaw via Vienna, and by the late 1840s had established himself as a major musical presence in the city as composer, performer and teacher [plate 1]. He frequented the fashionable salons of the day, including that of the Czartoryski family at the Hôtel Lambert, headed by Prince Adam Jerzy Czartoryski, leader of the exiled Polish community in Paris. His friends were many and varied: among musicians there were Bellini, Berlioz, Hallé, Kalkbrenner, Liszt and Mendelssohn; among painters, Delacroix and Ary Scheffer; among writers Adam Mickiewicz and George Sand. Chopin spent the winter of 1838–9 with Sand in Mallorca; subsequently she cosseted him in Paris and at her estate at Nohant. Here he wrote some of his finest compositions. But the ending of his relationship with Sand in 1847, and the political developments that deprived him of many of his aristocratic pupils who fled Paris, prompted his decision to move to Britain. In so doing, he was aided and abetted by Jane Stirling, a well-connected Scottish pupil who, with her sister Mrs Katherine Erskine, seemed ideally suited to help him in his transition to a new life on the English side of the Channel. Indeed, the Stirlings were to be almost over-solicitous, as Chopin was urged to give recitals in London and to travel round country seats in Scotland. His last concert in Paris took place on 26 February 1848 in the *Salons Pleyel*; two months later he left for London, which he reached on 21 April.[2]

LONDON AND SCOTLAND

The first of Chopin's two visits to Britain had taken place in 1837, when he spent ten days or so in London with Camille Pleyel, whose

CREDITS

Plates are reproduced by courtesy of the following:

Alec Cobbe, Cobbe Collection Trust: plate 18
(photo: John Challis)

© Fitzwilliam Museum, Cambridge: plate 8

Thomas Lloyd: plate 9

© Manchester City Galleries: plates 2, 12

Manchester Library and Information Service:
plates 4, 5, 12, 13, 14, 15, 18, 19

Middleton Civic Association: plate 6
(photo: Alan Seabright, 2003)

© National Portrait Gallery, London: plate 16

Private Collection: plates 1, 3, 11, 21

© Roehampton University Archives and Special
Collections: plate 5

© Royal College of Music, London: plate 20

© Royal Northern College of Music,
Manchester: cover, plates 22, 23, 24
(photos: Michael Pollard, 2008–10)

Plate 10 was taken in 2010 from
www.oldukphotos.com

INDEX